FATE SOMETIMES throws ordinary people into extraordinary circumstances. *Called* is the true and compelling story of a working woman, Lisa Jefferson, who suddenly one September morning found herself caught up in history, and who somehow found the inner strength and grace to play a role in one of the tragic yet inspiring stories of our time.

Charles Osgood
Host, CBS Sunday Morning
and The Osgood File, *CBS Radio*

LISA JEFFERSON stepped from her everyday life into an extraordinary moment on 9/11. She now shares with us her heart-wrenching experience and spiritual journey that followed in a valuable reflection on our national tragedy.

Catherine Crier
Former judge and Court TV host

CALLED is a compelling ear-witness account which will help us ALWAYS REMEMBER our first successful counterattack in this new war on our homeland. It is also a powerful witness as to the source of hope and strength sufficient to sustain us each day and in ALL situations . . . God and His Son Jesus Christ. Lisa Jefferson is a blessing to the Beamer clan and through *Called* she will be a blessing to you.

David and Peggy Beamer
Parents of Flight 93 hero Todd Beamer

LISA JEFFERSON'S story of her faith and beliefs during her harrowing Flight 93 experience fosters a spirituality that is the heart and soul of her book.

David Gerber
Producer, Flight 93 *movie*

AN UNFORGETTABLE BOOK about America's most unforgettable day. Lisa and my friend, Felicia, have done us all a favor as they take us deep into the tragedy where the true meaning of life is found in the midst of loss.

Dr. Joseph M. Stowell
Former president, Moody Bible Institute

ONE

PHONE

CALL...

AND A

LIFE IS

CHANGED

FOREVER.

"HELLO, MY NAME IS MRS. JEFFERSON.
I UNDERSTAND YOUR PLANE IS BEING HIJACKED . . . "

9:45 a.m., Flight 93, September 11, 2001

"HELLO, MY NAME IS MRS. JEFFERSON.
I UNDERSTAND YOUR PLANE IS BEING HIJACKED . . ."

9:45 a.m., Flight 93, September 11, 2001

by LISA D. JEFFERSON
and FELICIA MIDDLEBROOKS

NORTHFIELD PUBLISHING
CHICAGO

ISBN: 1-881273-75-X
ISBN-13: 978-1-881273-75-2

All Scripture quotations, unless otherwise indicated, are taken from the King James Version.

Scripture quotations marked NKJV are taken from the *New King James Version*. Copyright © 1982 by Thomas Nelson, Inc. Used by permission. All rights reserved.

Scripture quotations marked AMP are taken from *The Amplified Bible*. Copyright © 1965, 1987 by The Zondervan Corporation. Used by permission.

Library of Congress Cataloging-in-Publication Data

Jefferson, Lisa D., 1958-
  Called : "Hello, my name is Mrs. Jefferson, I understand your plane is being hijacked ..." : 9:45AM, Flight 93, September 11, 2001 / by Lisa D. Jefferson and Felicia Middlebrooks.
    p. cm.
  ISBN 1-881273-75-X
  1. Service (Theology) 2. Suffering—Religious aspects—Christianity. 3. Jefferson, Lisa D., 1958- 4. United Airlines Flight 93 Hijacking Incident, 2001. 5. September 11 Terrorist Attacks, 2001. 6. Beamer, Todd Morgan, 1968-2001. I. Middlebrooks, Felicia. II. Title.e.
  BT738.4.J44 2006
  973.93—dc222
                        2006011257

Edited by Elizabeth Cody Newenhuyse
Cover Designer: Charles Brock | The DesignWorks Group, Inc.
                www.thedesignworksgroup.com
Cover Image: Getty Images, Dimitri Vervits
Jacket Photo Credits:
        Photo of Lisa Jefferson: William Fletcher
        Photo of Felicia Middlebrooks: James Spada, Spada Photography
Interior Book Design: Julia Ryan

We hope you enjoy this book from Northfield Publishing. Our goal is to provide high-quality, thought-provoking books and products that connect truth to your real needs and challenges. For more information on other books and products written and produced from a biblical perspective, go to www.moodypublishers.com or write to:

Northfield Publishing
820 N. LaSalle Boulevard
Chicago, IL 60610

1 3 5 7 9 10 8 6 4 2

Printed in the United States of America

God's greatest joy is to be believed.
His greatest sorrow is when we doubt Him.

CONTENTS

IN MEMORIAM
UNITED AIRLINES FLIGHT 93

CREW
Captain Jason Dahl

First Officer Leroy Homer

Flight Attendant Lorraine G. Bay

Flight Attendant Sandra W. Bradshaw

Flight Attendant Wanda A. Green

Flight Attendant Cee Cee Ross Lyles

Flight Attendant Deborah A. Welsh

PASSENGERS

Christian Adams	Lauren Grandcolas
Todd Beamer	Donald Greene
Alan Beaven	Linda Gronlund
Mark Bingham	Richard Guadagno
Deora Bodley	Toshiya Kuge
Marion Britton	Hilda Marcin
Thomas Burnett	Waleska Martinez
William Cashman	Nicole Miller
Georgine Corrigan	Louis J. Nacke
Patricia Cushing	Jean Peterson
Joseph Deluca	Donald Peterson
Patrick Driscoll	Mark Rothenberg
Edward Felt	Christine Snyder
Jane Folger	John Talignani
Colleen Fraser	Honor Elizabeth Wainio
Andrew Garcia	Kristin White
Jeremy Glick	

ACKNOWLEDGMENTS

I dedicate this book to God, because through Him all things are possible. I also thank my husband Warren and our children, Lonye' and Warren II, for keeping me focused on what is truly important. I am grateful for the comfort you gave me during the stressful periods, and for never leaving my side.

I am also thankful for my mother and my late father, Bettie and Donald, for their unconditional support and love that inspires me to be the best person I can be every day.

Thanks to my mother-in-law Minnie and to Lizzie (Big Momma), for your endless support and continuous inspiration, and for keeping me mindful of Proverbs 3:5–6. To my sister and brother De'Brina and Lance Sr., I can't thank you enough for being my best friends. You are a constant source of love, and you're always there for me. My literary agent, the late Sherrill Chidiac, believed in this project from its inception. Thanks to Claudia Cross for picking up the literary torch, dotting all the i's and crossing the t's.

A special thanks to all my family and friends for standing with me through the good and the difficult times. Thank you, attorney Andrew Stroth, for your excellent and wise counsel.

To Felicia Middlebrooks, thank you for bringing this entire project together. To Pastor Ira J. Acree, thank you for your spiritual guidance, and to Anita Bingham, thank you for your unyielding spiritual strength. I am also grateful to Cheryl Wade, Edie McGee, and Kenneth Westbrook for being available on short notice. Thank you to the entire team at Moody Publishers. And finally, thank you to Lisa Beamer . . . my new friend, whose strength and faith I admire.

INTRODUCTION

Could anything good come out of September 11,
2001—possibly the darkest day in our recent history?

The tragedy of September 11th changed the course
of world history and forever changed American life as we
know it. Just as Ground Zero in lower Manhattan remains
a barren site that reminds us of our loss, so we struggle to
come to terms with the meaning of that day. But even as
we struggle to understand the ill will that so violently shook
our sense of freedom and safety, we have a choice. We can
live out our days trying to make sense of the senseless, or we
can trust God . . . and trust sometimes requires unanswered
questions.

But when tragedy strikes, we are not left without
options. We needn't feel abandoned and relegated to a
never-ending sense of powerlessness. We can still choose
how we respond. And when we choose to believe in the
awesome love and power of God, even amidst the darkest
circumstances, then we can know that our pain is a process
with a purpose. What we are forced to endure may not
look good. It may not feel good. But we know that God
can bring good out of it.

Throughout time, ever since Adam and Eve's forced exit from the garden of Eden, bad men with evil intentions have heaped their madness on humankind. Ours is a world where injustice sometimes overshadows what is right and righteous. Awful things sometimes happen to good people. But I believe God is still in control.

On the morning of that fateful day in our beloved America, God scheduled my role. When I rose early that morning, just a normal, everyday wife, mom, and worker, I was totally unaware that it was to be a day of collective grieving and great sorrow. I was totally unaware of the challenge God was going to send my way—or the lives He was going to place in my path.

He may have such a challenge for you—a call. It is my hope that, as I share my account of that day, you will be comforted, encouraged, and perhaps inspired. It is my sincere desire that you will come away with a deeper knowledge of God's character, and you'll understand that despite human tragedy, He still has a plan for each and every one of us. We can call it our assignment.

Are you ready?

Lisa D. Jefferson

"So do not fear, for I am with you;

Do not be dismayed, for I am your God.

I will strengthen you and help you;

I will uphold you with my righteous right hand."

Isaiah 41:10

JUST THINK

You're not here by chance, but by God's choosing.

His hand formed you and made you the person you are.

He compares you to no one else—you are one of a kind.

You lack nothing that His grace can't give you.

He has allowed you to be here at this time in history

to fulfill His special purpose for this generation.

Roy Lessin

called

TIMING IS EVERYTHING, BUT WHO HAS THE CLOCK?

MY NAME IS LISA D. JEFFERSON. You may have seen my face on network television, recounting an experience that has forever changed my heart and my once-quiet existence. You may have seen the experience—and me—portrayed on film, both in the theater and on television.

I was the Verizon Airfone supervisor who spent an incredible fifteen-minute audio journey with Todd Beamer, one of the heroes of United Airlines Flight 93. For those fifteen minutes, that telephone on the back of the airplane seat was literally a lifeline for him, as he used the last moments of his life to put himself before others, to fight for the preservation of America's liberty.

And those fifteen minutes changed me forever.

TODD BEAMER WAS KILLED when Flight 93 plunged into the ground in an abandoned strip mine in out-of-the-way Shanksville, Pennsylvania. In fact, there were no survivors. All seven crew members and thirty-three passengers perished—and they were all heroes.

I was there, at least in spirit. I could hear the cries and screams for help in the background, as Todd Beamer painted in vivid detail the occurrences aboard the plane on that awful day. I've accepted the fact that I'll never be the same. I've been interviewed more times than I can recall . . . radio, television, and print. I've consulted on movies and now, as the last surviving "voice of Flight 93," have been asked to assist in fund-raising efforts for a permanent memorial to honor those who fought for their country.

When I was first approached about writing a book chronicling my experience, I felt sure it was an unnecessary venture. I mean, what could I possibly say that I hadn't said before? It wasn't until I realized, through the wisdom of my church, as well as family and friends, that God had given me a compelling message.

An experience this deep and profound *should* be shared. My life has changed, and when you read this book and see September 11th through my eyes, your life may change as well. There are many facets of this national tragedy that will be examined for decades to come. This is my story, and this is the message I believe God wants to share with you, based on my experience.

IT WAS A TUESDAY MORNING. It started the way any other weekday morning would for me. I went to bed at a normal hour the night before, to ensure I would get plenty of sleep. I got up around 5:15 a.m. in our home in suburban Chicago. I'd packed the kids' lunches the night before. My son Warren was six at the time, and my daughter Lonye' was eight. They're pretty good about getting themselves dressed and in school mode, but preparing their lunches ahead always helps me glide through the morning routine, with one less task to perform.

The kids take a bus to school, and my mother was there to see them off. As usual, I left the house at around 6 a.m. At that time, I'd been a supervisor with Verizon Airfone (formerly known as GTE Airfone) in Oak Brook, Illinois, for the past seventeen years. I started at Airfone in 1984 and was there when the first phone was installed on an airplane. After six months I was promoted to team leader, and after another six months I became a supervisor. It felt like a good, secure company with opportunity to advance.

It was also where I met my husband, Warren. We were both city natives, he from the West Side of Chicago and I from the South Side. I was attracted to his can-do, take-charge kind of attitude—an attitude I would find myself relying on not only in the difficult post-9/11 days but throughout our marriage and in our parenting. Warren's the kind of man who steps up wherever he's needed, helping around the house and with the kids. He now owns his own property redevelopment business, but at the time he was a senior program manager for Verizon Airfone. Some mornings, we'd drive to work together, but on this day I went solo.

As I negotiated the early morning traffic on the Tri-State Tollway, radio on, sun shining, I felt at peace with my life. My children were healthy and happy; both my husband and I had good jobs; I was blessed with close friends and a loving extended family. Oh, it wasn't perfect—but it was *settled*.

I pulled into the parking lot at 6:45 a.m. Verizon Airfone is housed within a huge and beautiful corporate campus composed of seven tan brick office buildings, all with tinted glass. My particular building has three floors overlooking lush landscaping. Trees shade well-manicured lawns. There's even a pond, inhabited by two white swans, as well as mallards, and snowy egrets. It's really something to see. As I crossed the

As I crossed the parking lot almost without thinking, I of course was completely unaware that my tranquil, settled, everyday-Tuesday state of mind would be dramatically interrupted in less than two hours.

parking lot almost without thinking, I of course was completely unaware that my tranquil, settled, everyday-Tuesday state of mind would be dramatically interrupted in less than two hours.

I even remember what I wore that day: a black print skirt and matching top. I hadn't had a chance to grab breakfast at home. After taking the stairs to the second floor, I walked down the long corridor to my office, which looks out over tan, blue, and gray wraparound workstations. Each station has a computer and more telephones than a Jerry Lewis telethon.

There are file cabinets positioned on the sides of each desk. And we all share a host of printers and fax machines. I'd just settled in and reached for a banana I'd planned to eat with my instant oatmeal. I got a little distracted by some paperwork on my desk that needed tending to, so I put breakfast on hold.

My office was actually *in* the Verizon Airfone Call Center. There is a window inside that allows me to see all of the workstations. After a couple of hours of work, I walked outside my office to join a few other employees fixated on the radio news reports in the Call Center. I wanted to know what had suddenly captured everyone's attention. I was abruptly stopped by a Verizon Airfone representative under my authority. She was already on the job, wearing her headset and obviously talking to someone.

A call for help had come in at 8:45 a.m. central daylight time, answered by the Airfone rep, who beckoned frantically for me.

"Lisa!" she said with urgency, adjusting her headset. I was at her side in seconds. She was clearly traumatized.

"Oh my gosh!" said the representative. "You're for real, aren't you?" In just a few moments, I would learn that the person on the line was Todd Beamer. He was telling the representative that United Airlines Flight 93,

"Lisa!" she said with urgency, adjusting her headset. I was at her side in seconds. She was clearly traumatized.

bound for San Francisco from Newark, had been hijacked.

You may recall that in the aftermath of the World Trade Center disaster, there were reports that many of those who perished on the two planes that sliced through the towers were able to call their loved ones using cell phones. That was only possible because those planes were flying at a low altitude. But that was not the case with United Airlines Flight 93. The passengers aboard that plane made calls, some using the Airfones located in the back of the seats—and many of them called home. Todd Beamer was the exception, and his call came directly through to the Verizon Airfone Call Center. He simply dialed "0" from the phone nestled in the back of the headrest on the seat in front of him.

I'VE ALWAYS BEEN what some might call "reserved." Those who know me say I don't excite easily. The only time I remember really falling apart was when our daughter, Lonye', was two. She had been born with a cyst on her brain, and when she was two she found her way through a guard gate

I had left open. She fell, hit her head on the floor, and was unconscious. I blamed myself for not locking the gate, and I lost it.

She had surgery when she was six, and now she's fine. Looking back, I wonder if that trauma was, in a sense, preparation for what God was going to send my way that Tuesday morning.

THERE ARE PROCEDURES we follow in the event of an emergency. The first thing we needed to ascertain was the flight information, the name of the airline, and the routing of the plane. All that we learned would be turned over to the Airfone Operations Surveillance Center (AOSC) for processing. The Surveillance Center is responsible for contacting the authorities in emergencies. (I later discovered that when the AOSC called the local 911 operator to report the incident that the operator's name was Lisa.)

Initially, the Airfone rep was able to give me basic flight information as she muted her phone, while speaking with the caller. I tried to contact the

Surveillance Center on another phone, but when there was no answer, I ran over to the AOSC next door. Time was at a premium. I knew lives were probably at stake, so I had to act quickly.

Having memorized the flight numbers, I informed officials that a United Airlines plane had been hijacked, and then I returned to the representative in the Call Center. There she sat, completely frozen. I realized this call was more than she could handle, but I wasn't certain I was prepared to handle it either. As a supervisor I had not spoken directly to a customer in nearly two years. Furthermore, our department had no prior training for *this* type of emergency. There was no protocol, no corporate manual to use for guidance. I had to rely on my own wisdom. I spoke calmly to the Airfone rep.

"I'll finish the call; you can move to another station."

I sat down in the tan cloth chair, not realizing I'd be riveted there for the next hour. I gazed down briefly at the gray, tan, blue, and mauve speckled carpeting as I put her headset on. I took a deep breath.

"Hello, my name is Mrs. Jefferson. I understand your plane is being hijacked?"

"Yes," the man said, quite calmly.

"Can you explain to me in detail exactly what's taking place?"

The caller began to honor the request, but his voice was devoid of any stress. In fact, he sounded so tranquil it made me begin to doubt the authenticity and urgency of his call. The Call Center had never had a hijacking reported. We've had our share of scares, like bomb threats (none of them legitimate), and passengers becoming ill on the plane. Generally, the Call Center gets bombarded with inquisitive customers or children playing with the phones.

While I spoke with the caller, I watched a monitor that showed me the airline, the time, and information confirming that the plane was still in flight. This was real. The more the caller spoke, the more I realized the

The more the caller spoke, the more I realized the gravity of the situation he and his fellow passengers were facing.

gravity of the situation he and his fellow passengers were facing.

"Three people have hijacked the plane. Two have taken over the cockpit, and they're flying the plane," he said in a matter-of-fact tone.

I was concentrating so deeply that I hardly noticed that my colleagues in the Call Center had begun to gather around my station. I could hear intermittent conversations: Someone in the background said, "These are suicide attempts—they are intentionally taking those planes down!" It was then that I learned that two planes had actually felled the World Trade Center Towers, but I remained intensely focused on one voice—that of the man on the phone.

I knew that Flight 93 could be in real trouble, but at this juncture I had no idea the hijacking incidents were tragically and inextricably linked, part of a terrible plot. (Interestingly, it has since been suggested that Zacarias Moussaoui, recently on trial for his role in the 9/11 attacks, was originally supposed to be one of the hijackers on Flight 93.)

My colleagues could not hear the man speaking with me. They could only hear my responses to him and my inquiries. The man continued to describe his surroundings.

A note was then handed to me by someone. The FBI wanted me to try to determine if the caller could figure out the nationality of the hijackers. I never got a chance to ask that question, because *the caller* was providing a steady stream of other vital information. I didn't want to carelessly cut him off, break his focus, and possibly make him nervous.

"Two of the three people taking over the plane have knives. They've locked themselves into the cockpit," he said. It was later determined there were actually four hijackers. Later, when I was asked to testify at the Moussaoui trial, the number of the hijackers was a vital piece of information the government sought.

"One of them has what looks like a bomb strapped to his waist, with a red belt. He's standing in First Class. They've ordered everyone to sit down."

My breathing grew rapid, but I tried to remain calm. I felt as if I were having an out-of-body experience. I felt ill . . . sickened by what I was hearing. I didn't want to be there; I wished someone else could take over. But my voice never reflected that. I knew this was not a fantasy or a dream, but it was almost as if time slowed—and I was trying to respond to this crisis in real time. The caller continued.

"The flight attendants were standing. The hijackers ordered them to sit, and one just happened to sit next to me. That's how I'm getting my information."

I wrote as he spoke. I wanted to make sure the notes I passed on to the Call Center were accurate and timely. Those notes would later be examined by the authorities. (I had not had a chance to press the switch in my office that initiates the taping of a conversation.)

"There are two people lying on the floor in First Class. I think they're hurt," he said, his voice remaining even.

I then asked him if he could tell me anything more about the people lying on the floor of the plane.

"I can't tell if they're dead or alive. The flight attendant next to me says it's the pilot and the co-pilot."

It was then that a fear rose up in me such as I'd never known before. I prayed silently in my mind and heart, not really knowing what to ask God. I felt as though my faith was on the line, and I was compelled to remain steadfast and unmovable. I realized, with a dread certainty, that this hijacking was linked to the tragedy in New York.

The caller told me that the terrorist standing in the aisle had pulled the curtain in First Class, shrouding their view. He could no longer see what was going on.

By now, a sizeable crowd had gathered around my workstation as word of the emergency situation spread through other departments. I was keenly aware of the workers' presence, but by the grace of God, I managed to block them all out.

I wasn't even aware of their body heat as they pressed up against the cubicle. As odd as it may sound, it was as if no one else were there except me and *the caller*. It was almost as if we were just sitting there, talking. I never had to tell those around me to *shush*. They were clearly in shock, but never spoke above a whisper. It wasn't until I stood up that I became truly aware of the throngs of people around me.

called

CHAPTER TWO

SOMEONE IS LISTENING

MEANWHILE, MY HUSBAND WARREN was upstairs in the Verizon Airfone complex in another department. The television set in his office only had a six-inch screen, just big enough for personal viewing. But on *this* day, colleagues were drawn to it like a magnet. Today was an exception. Instead of just a few people trickling in and out of his office, there was a standing-room-only crowd. All eyes were glued to the television as they watched the nightmare in New York City unfold. Warren was completely unaware that downstairs, his wife was playing a small part in the day's dramatic events.

"Mrs. Jefferson, are you there?" the caller asked, his voice slightly elevated.

"Yes sir, I'm here . . . and I'm going to stay with you."

"Do you know what the hijackers want, Mrs. Jefferson? Is it money, ransom, or what?"

I have since wondered how much Todd knew about what was going on in New York and Washington DC. In the context of that time period, a "hijacking" usually meant that the hijackers wanted something —and once they got it the passengers would be released. Nobody, really, could dream of a suicide mission.

We now know, of course, that other Flight 93 passengers had been making calls; later information shows that some may have been warned. I will never know for certain how much Todd was aware of. At *that* particular moment, though, it was clear that the man on the flight was aware of the danger he faced, but he obviously believed there was a remedy—and there was no reason to think he and the other passengers would not be rescued.

"I'm sorry, sir. I don't know what the hijackers are asking for. Can you tell me how many people are on the flight?"

I could hear him whisper to the flight attendant sitting beside him.

"The flight attendant says there are ten people in the front, twenty-seven in the back, and five flight attendants."

"Do you know if there are any children aboard the flight?"

"None that I can see, Mrs. Jefferson."

"Well, I want you to know that all the appropriate authorities have been notified, and at this point if you believe your life is in jeopardy while talking to me—just put the phone down, but try not to hang it up."

I wanted *the caller* to know that I could hear what was going on in the background. I could hear him breathing.

"Oh, Mrs. Jefferson, I can still talk to you." It was at this point that I finally asked him his name.

"I'm Todd Beamer from Cranbury, New Jersey," he responded. As we continued a little small talk, the plane began flying erratically. Todd raised his voice a bit. Then I heard raw panic.

"Oh my God, we're going down! We're going down! Jesus help us!"

My body chilled as I heard Todd's cries. I was shaking on the inside, though I appeared calm to my colleagues. Physically, I felt ill and helpless. But spiritually, I remained calm. It was a supernatural calm I'd never experienced before. An overwhelming sense of peace enveloped me. I knew God was with me, *and* with Todd. I wanted to do more to help Todd and the other passengers and crew, but I couldn't. At that moment, I felt as though I was on the plane myself. I was visualizing everything that was going on as Todd and I talked . . . and as I heard screams and audible gasps in the background. It was an experience that's almost indescribable.

In my spirit, I cried out and prayed for God's help. *What do I say?* I secretly wished someone else would rescue me and take over this call. *Why me, Lord?* Why did I have to be the person chosen to be

the conduit between these helpless passengers
and a team of rescuers who never got to complete
their mission?

While these questions
were going through my head,
I began to hear profoundly
disturbing sounds coming
from the cabin of the plane.
What was that? Then I realized
what I was hearing: screams,
bloodcurdling screams. These
innocents aboard Flight 93
were crying out for their very
lives, *and I couldn't help them.* The phone was
my only point of contact, and no one could bear
witness to what I heard except Todd and his
fellow passengers.

*These innocents
aboard Flight 93
were crying out
for their very lives,
and I couldn't
help them.*

Though my colleagues were as statues around
me, listening to what I was saying to Todd Beamer,
they could not know the horror of the sounds of
desperation that I heard. I will carry those sounds to
my grave. They are not easily forgotten. The shrill
screams of fear, the human cries of terror and

disbelief. These were people forced to suffer at the hands of tyrants who commandeered their flight. Their lives had been rudely interrupted, and I was to play a role in saving those lives. At least that was my hope.

The commotion and screaming had not ceased, and I just wanted to yank my headset off and throw in the towel. This was too much for me. But I knew I was Todd's lifeline. I couldn't leave him, and I knew God wouldn't leave me. I never told Todd that I was just as nervous and afraid as he was. I just kept talking to him, trying to keep him calm. Just then, I heard a man in the background shouting.

"Oh my God, Jesus! Oh my God!"

Then I heard a woman screaming. It was a piercing scream. We all recognize a yell or a cry of pain. But this was different. It was clear these were desperate, anguished cries for help, from people clinging to a sheer thread of life. A man with a baritone voice near Todd then said, "Oh no! No! God, *no!" What was happening on that plane?*

Then Todd's voice could be heard, and he sounded calmer.

"No, wait. We're coming back up. I think we're okay now." Then Todd asked, "Would you say the Lord's Prayer with me?"

"Yes, of course, Todd." Then we prayed.

"Our Father who art in heaven, hallowed be thy name. Thy kingdom come. Thy will be done in earth, as it is in heaven. Give us this day our daily bread. And forgive us our trespasses, as we forgive those who trespass against us. And lead us not into temptation, but deliver us from evil: For thine is the kingdom, and the power, and the glory, forever, Amen."

"Jesus help me," said Todd. "I just wanted to talk to someone, and if I don't make it through this, will you do me a favor? Would you tell my wife and family how much I love them?"

"Of course I'll do that for you, Todd. Would you like me to try to reach your wife and patch her call through?"

"I just wanted to talk to someone, and if I don't make it through this, will you do me a favor?"
Todd asked.

"No, no. I don't want to upset her unnecessarily. She's expecting our third child in January, and if I don't have to upset her with any bad news, then I'd rather not."

I CAN'T EXPLAIN THE MYRIAD OF EMOTIONS I was feeling at this time. Here I was, talking with a man I had never met, a man who was obviously passionate about his life and his wife and family. His fate, I knew, was still hanging in the balance; and I happened to be the one *chosen* to talk with him, while he unknowingly stood poised between his full, young life—and eternity.

All I could do was hope that I was responding in a way that was right and proper—and in a way that honored God.

called

CHAPTER THREE

SILENCE OF THE INNOCENTS

IT SEEMED AS IF TODD AND I WERE OLD FRIENDS, though I hardly knew him. I believe crises have a way of transcending time and quickly bridging gaps. All that mattered was our humanity. We were kindred spirits. This was a conversation between two followers of Christ, both desperately seeking God. The image that comes to me was of Todd in a ship on a storm-tossed sea—even though he was thousands of feet in the air. I, on the ground, was his lifeline on the shore.

"I have a beautiful wife and two little boys, David and Andrew," he said. Todd then gave me his home phone number. The brief calm was interrupted.

"Oh my God, we're turning around! We're turning around!" My heart raced as I listened to Todd.

"I think we're going north, but at this point, who knows *where* we're going!"

Then:

"Lisa!" Todd shouted.

"Yes," I answered.

"Oh, that's my wife's name."

"Todd, that's *my* name too."

"Oh, you're kidding."

The plane began to fly erratically again. *What was going on?*

"Lisa, Lisa!"

"I'm still here, Todd, and I'm not going anywhere. I'll be on this phone as long as you are."

"A few of us passengers are getting together. I think we're going to jump the guy with the bomb!"

"Are you sure that's what you want to do, Todd?"

"Yes. I'm going to have to go out on faith, because at this point, I don't have much of a choice."

"Well, if that's your decision, Todd, I'm behind you and I support your decision."

At this point, we were both hoping that the plane could be landed without incident. There was still reason to hope. Todd and I just kept talking about the plane being landed safely, and we both agreed not to give up. He then apparently turned away from the phone.

"Are you ready?"

I couldn't hear the other person's response.

"Okay, let's roll!"

I HELD THE PHONE LINE OPEN for approximately fifteen more minutes. I constantly called Todd's name, hoping that he or someone else would come and pick up the phone. I sat there calling, "Todd, Todd. Are you there?"

No response. This went on for what seemed like hours. I was calling to Todd, but he was not responding. Then came the news: United Airlines Flight 93 had just crashed in Pennsylvania.

"Lisa," one of my colleagues said gently.

"Lisa, release the phone line. That was Todd's plane."

One of the engineers had been tracing the call from the moment Todd phoned for help. The call from Todd's end in Pennsylvania went silent.

I felt as though my breath completely left my body. It was as though all the blood rushed to my feet. I didn't feel like flesh and bone; I felt like lead. I couldn't move. I hadn't given up hope. With the headset still on, I called out again.

"Todd, Todd! Can you hear me? Are you there, Todd?"

"Lisa, release the phone line now."

"No, no, just wait a minute," I said. "Someone might still be there!"

Still I sat, in the midst of a crowded room and a deafening silence. Then the tears began to flow. Not just my own, but from the weary eyes of my colleagues standing around me.

"Lisa, the radio station just reported it. Flight 93 is down. Please, Lisa, you can release the phone line now," said a male colleague who was visibly shaken.

I knew it was over. I knew that brave man on the other side of the phone had perished, and a part of me went with him. I knew that all those innocents were gone. Every time I called out to Todd during those fifteen minutes of silence, I prayed.

I knew that brave man on the other side of the phone had perished, and a part of me went with him.

"Please God, save these people. Please God, save my friend Todd."

It was as if time stood still. I felt such sadness, a depth of grief I'd never known before. I felt as if I'd failed, though I did all that was humanly possible. I had been standing on the shore with the lifeline in my hand. Had I let it go?

called

CHAPTER FOUR

THE EMPTY SKY

WARREN LATER TOLD ME that he and several colleagues were glued to the television in his third-floor office when the telephone rang.

"Warren, you need to come downstairs immediately," said his coworker, sounding insistent, almost somber. Warren said he initially questioned the importance of the request. After all, what could be more relevant than the unfolding of a national tragedy? After several exchanges between them, Warren finally realized that *something* legitimately needed his attention. Maybe Lisa was sick, he thought. And so he complied and went downstairs to the Call Center.

I was hanging up the phone and removing my headset when Warren arrived. I was shaking and didn't feel much like talking. After visually canvassing the room, seeing Warren's face and the expressions on the faces of my colleagues, I could see that everyone was deeply concerned about me. Warren later said I looked like I was in shock, standing frozen at the desk. Tears began to well up in my eyes.

"Lisa, are you okay?" Warren asked quietly.

"Yeah, I'm okay," I answered.

He didn't seem convinced by my tone. Warren looked very worried and didn't seem to know what to do. I knew he didn't even have the full story yet. I felt emotionally drained. I stood up and walked zombie-like into my office. My husband knew enough not to speak about *the incident*, so he just stayed at my side, giving me unspoken support. When he finally left to return to his department, two other colleagues offered me comfort and prayed with me.

I remained at the office until 1p.m. That's when the Bush White House and the U.S. military declared a nationwide ground halt at airports around the country. You might remember in those eerie days immediately following 9/11 how quiet the skies were. No planes were allowed to take off, and those that were still in the air were ordered to land.

I was still in my office when I received word that I was to go to the AOSC, where FBI agents waited on the line, wanting to talk to me. None of the agents were physically in the building at that time. They had all maintained contact via telephone. There were three agents that I was aware of. They were from New York, Chicago, and Washington DC.

It was vital that these agents conduct what was called a "post-crisis interview." I was feeling very drained, but my husband's presence helped me to cope. He was with me during the interrogation,

As you can imagine, it's frightening to get caught up in the web of grave matters of national security.

and I was very thankful, because as you can imagine, as an ordinary citizen it's frightening to get caught up in the web of grave matters of national security— even when your information is aiding in the effort to protect our security.

The FBI agents asked me scores of questions. They said they were grateful for my vivid recollections. Then came the big question: How long were you on the phone with Todd Beamer? I told them I had no idea. It seemed like a short time. When the agents asked me for a ballpark guess, I told them about fifteen minutes, and that's what the media picked up.

Right then, however, the story in the media was the furthest thing from my mind. In a corner of Pennsylvania, a field smoldered and swarmed with emergency personnel. And I felt as empty as the skies overhead.

called

CHAPTER FIVE

HOLD MY HAND

AFTER THE INITIAL POST-CRISIS INTERVIEW was over, I went back to my office. Warren and I spoke several more times over the next hour or so, in person and over the phone. I was grateful that we worked for the same company and were in the same building. I don't know what I would have done without his support.

The Call Center was beginning to look like a ghost town. Employees were told to go home, following the nationwide ground halt. A few remaining colleagues entered my office to check on me. I knew they were concerned, and I was confused and numb . . . but still very grateful.

Two Verizon Airfone workers plopped down in the swivel chairs in my office. Another worker got a glass of water for me. No one knew what to say. For a time, we all sat there in silence.

"Lisa, are you okay?" The silence was finally broken. I looked up at my colleague and tried to force a smile.

"Lisa, you're not *okay*." My coworkers could see through my thin veneer of composure.

"Lisa, you're *not* okay." They could see through my thin veneer of composure. And I didn't have the energy to dispute that assessment. I looked over at my desk. The oatmeal that I'd planned to have for breakfast that morning was still in its original beige pouch, untouched. The banana was left unpeeled. That was the first of many missed meals. I didn't eat anything for days afterward. I couldn't. I had no appetite, and the stress I was experiencing was about to get worse . . . much worse.

I finally decided there was nothing more I could do, and I should probably just drive home.

My spine felt as though it was in traction. I was stiff, numb, and dazed, like some sort of preprogrammed android. I assured my husband Warren that I would be okay, but he insisted on trailing me home. I didn't put up a fight. I didn't have the energy to challenge him.

I got into my car and switched on the radio. Finally, I couldn't take any more of the audio horror. The next thing I knew, I was sitting in my car in front of my suburban Chicago home. I don't even remember driving. Warren made sure I got into the house. Then he went to the bus stop to pick up our two children.

I walked into my home through the garage and directly into the first-floor family room. The house *seemed* quiet, until I became aware of a low buzzing sound. There, beside the oak-trimmed fireplace, the 35-inch television set was on. I hardly noticed my mother sitting on the leather sofa, with her chin resting on the palm of her hand, deeply engrossed in CNN's coverage of the tragedy. I glanced up at the black ceiling fan. Then I looked at my oak kitchen table and matching cabinets, as

if I were seeing them for the first time. Clearly, I was not myself. I didn't know *who* I was—and I was too sad and paralyzed to care.

I didn't know who I was—and I was too sad and paralyzed to care.

"Hi, honey. What are you doing home?"

"Hi, Mom; they sent us home early today." My mother was watching the television, and the television was watching *me*. I couldn't concentrate. I knew I was in shock. I couldn't feel anything.

"Mom, we got an emergency call today, and it was from one of the planes. . . . "

My voice trailed off. It was clear my mother wasn't listening. She seemed oblivious to my non-functional and numbed state. She was too deeply engrossed in the news coverage. That was okay with me. I was drained and really found myself incapable of telling her about what I'd experienced.

I went upstairs to my bedroom to get out of my work clothes. When I returned to the family room downstairs, my mother was still seated in the same position, mesmerized by what she was seeing and hearing. Just then, the doorbell rang. It was a close family friend named Jerome. He lived in a neighboring suburb and happened to be driving in the area. He decided to stop at our home, after seeing Warren's car parked in the driveway, which was unusual for this time of day. Jerome, of course, was unaware of my ordeal at work. I welcomed him into our home, saying nothing about my experience.

I was on the phone with my sister De'Brina when the call-waiting beeped. It was the FBI. "I'll call you back," I told my sister. I went to another part of the house for some privacy. The agent and I discussed the events of the day, and I was told to maintain secrecy. In fact, he stressed the importance of keeping the matter under wraps. The agent provided me with a host of telephone numbers to call, should I remember any additional details I might not have revealed earlier. He also said I could contact Lisa Beamer—but later that week.

Meanwhile, I still had job duties to think about. As a Verizon Airfone supervisor, it was my responsibility to call everyone on the second shift, to tell them not to come to work because of the

national tragedy. Thankfully, the list wasn't long.
There were only eight employees I had to reach.
I spoke with each of them briefly, never revealing to
them any facet of my dreadful experience. I simply
stuck to the facts, and told them the Call Center
would be closed until further notice.

Looking back now, I can't fathom how
I managed to keep my presence of mind. I'm sure
I was being sustained only by the grace of God.

Fortunately, word about the terrorist attacks
had spread quickly, and most of the employees were
already well aware of the crisis. I knew I couldn't
speak in detail with anyone concerning the active
investigation. I was under FBI orders not to do so.
I was determined to honor that.

I RETURNED TO THE FAMILY ROOM where Jerome
and my mother were watching CNN. They were
almost in a trance-like state. Jerome looked up and
asked if I was okay. I guess he surmised from my
expression that something wasn't quite right. But
I never shared the grueling hours I'd spent at the

Call Center. I mumbled something and just sat there with them, motionless and silent. At about this time, Warren returned home from the bus stop with the children.

Warren struck up a conversation with Jerome, but I could see he was distracted. He was still worried about me. He later told me he had an uneasy feeling in his spirit that I was deeply troubled, but he said whatever trauma I was experiencing, I hid it well.

I encouraged him to go on to his other job. At the time, Warren was doing some consulting work at O'Hare Airport. He didn't want to go, but he honored my request—reluctantly. It was about 3:45 p.m. Warren and Jerome left the house together.

"Momma, something bad happened today!" My daughter Lonye' was very excited as she tried to get my attention.

"The teacher explained what was going on!" Within moments, the children joined my mother in the family room—all of them gathered around the television as if it were a campfire. Warren

called every hour on the hour to see if I was okay.
I reassured him that I was.

My mother spends a lot of time with us,
helping to get the kids off to school and back home
again. I was very grateful she was around on this
particular day. I don't know what I would have
done without her comforting presence in my home
. . . especially then.

Nightfall came, and I welcomed it. I've heard
it said that Tuesday is the most productive day of
the week for the American worker. I would have
begged to differ, had I had the energy. I was just
glad Tuesday was over.

called

CHAPTER SIX

TWO HURTING LISAS

TUESDAY, SEPTEMBER 11, 2001 was over. Now I, along with the rest of America, would have to face the morning after—the *world* after. I remember going to bed, but I don't remember sleeping. My mind was too preoccupied with the events of the horrible day before.

As hard as it may be to fathom, I returned to work Wednesday, September 12th, as if all were well. The office was buzzing all day long. People gathered in small groups to talk about *the tragedy*. Air travel was almost nonexistent, so the workload was pretty light. Colleagues came to me, asking if I was all right.

What was I supposed to say? Should I have told them I was a nervous wreck? Should I have told them how bad I felt that I couldn't stop Flight 93 from plunging into the ground?

Should I tell them how I cried out to my God—asking whether I did the right thing? Did I do enough? Was there something I should have said to Todd Beamer that I didn't? Instead, I just told everyone I was okay. Not fine, but just okay.

THURSDAY, SEPTEMBER 13TH I returned to work, and once again, it was the same drill. Scores of people filed through my office, genuinely concerned. And again, I'd reply politely.

"Yeah, I'm okay. Really I am." By now, I'd actually managed to convince myself that I *really* was okay.

By Friday, the inquiries ceased. I privately congratulated myself for convincing people that although the crisis had deeply affected me, I could resume some semblance of normalcy. I'd even fooled myself. Within a couple of days, I was to receive a rude awakening about my own reality.

I got a call from my director at Verizon Airfone. The FBI had apparently contacted him with word that it was okay for Lisa Beamer to receive the message that I'd spoken with Todd in the last moments of the ill-fated flight. This wasn't just *any* Friday. Ironically, it was the birthdate of both my husband *and* my son. But there would be no birthday celebrations. The occasion was overshadowed by our grief.

I wrestled with what to tell Lisa Beamer. "Lisa, this is Lisa," didn't sound right.

I spoke with my director and asked for advice on how best to make the call to Lisa Beamer. I was afraid . . . unsure. I tried to put myself in this poor, pregnant young widow's shoes, and there was little comfort in pondering the task that lay ahead.

I wrestled with what to tell this young woman. Should I say, "Lisa, I spoke with your husband, Todd, on Tuesday"? That didn't sound

quite right. Neither did, "Lisa, hi, this is Lisa."
I was in a quandary. My director helped to ease
my discomfort.

"Lisa, United Airlines has a support group.
Maybe we should contact them and ask for some
advice."

A letter was quickly fashioned and sent by
fax to United Airlines grief counselors, who were
already working with Lisa Beamer. The letter
informed Mrs. Beamer, that I, Lisa Jefferson, had
a message for her from her husband, whenever
she felt ready to talk. The letter included contact
information for my home and work. The grief
counselors delivered the letter to Lisa Beamer.
Little did I know she'd have possession of that
letter in less than eight hours. And little did I
know she would not sleep after reading it.

I WILL NEVER FORGET SATURDAY, SEPTEMBER 15TH.
I have a standing appointment at the hair salon at
7:00 a.m. on Saturdays. It was nearly 10:00 a.m.,
and my daughter and I were just returning home.
As we walked in the door the phone was ringing.

Warren rushed to the top of the stairs with a shocked look on his face. He got a glimpse of the caller ID.

"Lisa!" He paused. *"Beamer."*

Silence. Warren still looked stunned. I had to say something. The phone was still ringing.

"Warren, it must be a mistake!" I yelled upstairs as I took my jacket off. "We just sent the letter yesterday."

The phone was still ringing. I thought perhaps it was a call from United Airlines, and they'd gotten the wrong Lisa. I didn't want to pick up the phone. I was in the kitchen and Warren was upstairs in the bedroom calling for me to pick up the phone. As I reached the top of the stairs, Warren had already picked it up.

All Warren had said was, *Beamer.* I joined Warren in our bedroom. Finally, I gathered enough courage to answer.

"Hello."

I could hear a woman's trembling voice. She was trying to speak, but was obviously crying. I heard the woman mutter something and then " . . . Beamer."

That's when it dawned on me—that's what Warren was trying to tell me. This *was* Lisa Beamer. I quickly glanced at the caller ID, and sure enough, it read *L. Beamer*.

"I understand you spoke to my husband?"

"Yes, I did." I paused. "Are you ready to talk?"

"Yes," she said timidly.

I then recounted the entire conversation, as best I could remember. But I realized as I was speaking that *I* wasn't really ready to talk. It had only been four days since the air tragedy. But we talked just the same. It was a cathartic experience for us both.

"Lisa, your husband really loved you. He was very concerned about you and the children, and your unborn baby. He asked me to tell you how much he loves you, and that everything will work out fine."

I could hear her crying, and I was wondering what I'd do and how I'd feel if I were bearing her pain. I learned in our talk that Lisa is a Christian. This was our common denominator, and I am sure that without question, God ordered our connection. I could not possibly console Lisa Beamer with anything other than the Word of God. Thankfully, because she was already a believer, she was able to freely receive God's comfort.

"Thank you for being there for Todd. You're a rock and pillar of strength," she said.

It was a lovely compliment from one so grief-stricken, but I didn't feel very strong in my own power. I knew that the strength I exhibited was clearly from God. I felt a spiritual calling. I knew God had placed me in the Beamers' lives "for such a time as this."

Lisa Beamer explained that she had received the faxed letter late Friday evening, within minutes after it was sent via United Airlines. She said she couldn't sleep because she was so anxious to call Saturday morning to hear what her husband wanted to tell her.

Warren sat beside me on our bed. I was relieved to have his support and comfort. Ironically, Lisa Beamer told me her brother was sitting with her in her bedroom as well, as she placed the call to me. She said she couldn't phone without having her brother there to help her endure the ordeal. I totally understood.

So there we sat. The two Lisas, both grieving, both hanging on to each other's every word. She told me about her two little boys, and she worried about how they might cope without Daddy.

We talked about her pregnancy . . . and being a mother myself, I felt a deep sorrow that she would have to endure delivery without the support of her husband, and it was my prayer that, God willing, she would give birth to a healthy child despite her circumstances. I was pleased to hear Lisa Beamer speak of her close family ties. She assured me that they were all standing by her and were each ready and willing to assume whatever role was necessary in helping her rear her children without Todd . . . although she'd never imagined she'd ever be without him. Lisa and I made a pact to keep in touch.

"I'm keeping you in my prayers, Lisa. If you need me, you have my number. I hope you'll call. We can just talk if you like," I said to her, sounding almost maternal.

"I'd like that, Lisa. I really would like that. I can't wait to meet you."

There were more tears.

Lisa Beamer then asked if I wouldn't mind speaking with a newspaper reporter from Pennsylvania. The reporter had been talking with her about her husband and the last moments of Flight 93. I was a little uneasy about the prospect, because I had never spoken with the media. I was inexperienced and didn't know how to respond to a reporter, but I obliged and told Lisa Beamer I'd speak with the man. Later that afternoon I did. I knew God had called me to *serve* this woman and her family. And I believe that's what living for God really is: serving others. My heart was breaking for her. Lisa and I spoke for about twenty minutes.

The Jefferson household received nearly a hundred calls from all over the world that first weekend after 9/11.

AFTER I SPOKE AT LENGTH WITH THE REPORTER that afternoon, I might as well have taken out a newspaper ad, offering interviews. The phone in our home rang incessantly from Saturday afternoon through late Sunday evening. We received scores of calls from reporters, literally from all over the world—wanting firsthand accounts of that awful day. Our ordinary, sometimes-mundane home life had been turned upside down. It became so difficult to handle that we finally had to just unplug the phones so our family could get some sleep. Eventually, Verizon's human resources department stepped in to field calls. The Jefferson household received nearly a hundred calls in that weekend alone.

called

CHAPTER SEVEN

A TIME FOR TEARS

"LISA! DID YOU SEE the newspapers this morning?"
The call Sunday morning was from an excited friend,
Valita, who was well acquainted with my ordeal.

"That man, that man you spoke with . . . his
picture is on the cover of the *Chicago Sun-Times*.
And there are the other passengers from Flight 93!"
Warren offered to go and pick up the Sunday papers,
but I told him not to bother. I immediately got
dressed and drove to our neighborhood Walgreens
drugstore to buy the papers. I wanted to see for
myself. I *needed* to see for myself. I rushed into the

drugstore, and there on the newspaper stand was the face of Todd Beamer.

This was the man I'd spoken with, connected with. Before now, I'd never seen a picture of him. When Lisa Beamer and I spoke the day before, I asked her to send me a picture of her husband.

"Of course I'll send you a picture, but what do you *think* he looks like?" Lisa Beamer asked me, trying to lighten our conversation.

"I'd imagined him wearing something white, and he has dark hair," I said tentatively, wondering if I might be right.

"Oh, he *does* have dark hair, and he *was* wearing a white dress shirt, with a dark business suit."

When Lisa Beamer confirmed the picture I already had in my mind's eye on that fateful day as I spoke with her husband, I knew he was with the angels in heaven.

The photos of Todd and the rest of the victims of Flight 93 had just been released to the media. I

Here are the Jeffersons! My husband, Warren, and I (inset); and in the large photo, son Warren II, Warren and I, and daughter Lonye'.

(TOP) *It's strange to see yourself being played by an actress in a movie! But I thought Monnae Michaell did a good job portraying me in the A&E movie, "Flight 93"— the highest-rated show on the channel ever.*

(RIGHT)*The Verizon offices in Oak Brook, Illinois—where I took "the call."*

A panoramic view of the temporary Flight 93 memorial in Shanksville, Pennsylvania. I would like to go there sometime.

This is an actual Airfone salvaged from the crash site.

In memory of those who gave their lives—gifts at the Flight 93 memorial.

An ice sculpture, in honor of those who fell on 9/11.

I was honored by the American Red Cross in 2003.

In Washington D.C., with my Congressman, Jesse Jackson Jr., and Catherine Crier of Court TV. Warren and I were invited to Court TV's "Everyday Heroes" awards program.

With former Chicago Police Superintendent
Terry Hillard at the Crime Stopper Awards ceremony.

(TOP): *Yes, that is me with former President Bill Clinton and the Rev. Jesse Jackson at a Rainbow PUSH Coalition event.*

(BOTTOM): *The U.S. Capitol—which may well have been saved by the Flight 93 heroes.*

It was a thrill to meet Todd Beamer's parents, David and Peggy, and his sister Michele.

(TOP): *I met two of the* Flight 93 *film actors on Larry King Live: Ty Olsson (left) played Mark Bingham, another hero; and Brennan Elliott portrayed Todd Beamer.*

(BOTTOM): *With (from left) producer David Gerber; Larry King; Brennan Elliott; Alice Hoglan, the mother of Mark Bingham; and Ty Olsson.*

I was invited to the 2004 dedication of Wheaton College's Beamer Center, a student center named after alumnus Todd. Lisa Beamer, shown with her daughter, Morgan, spoke at the program. (The mural depicts Todd and his two sons.)

David Beamer sings the National Anthem at a Wheaton game that weekend.

The flag marks the actual Flight 93 impact site.
Only family members are allowed on the site,
about a quarter-mile from the memorial.

Celebrating heroes.

had not yet received a picture from Lisa Beamer—
and there he was on the front page of the newspaper.

This was Todd Beamer, the father of two
beautiful little boys and a darling pregnant wife,
who shared my name. This was Todd Beamer, the
face of the courageous man who boldly bore witness
of his faith in Christ. I gazed at the paper. I wasn't
even cognizant of the length of time I stood there at
the newspaper stand. I just stood because I couldn't
move. I felt myself beginning to unravel. I knew
I was coming undone . . . and there wasn't a thing
I could do about it.

Todd Beamer. I just kept calling his name
over and over in my mind. My eyes welled up with
tears. My vision became cloudy. I could no longer
see his face, nor the faces of his fellow passengers,
with clarity. There they were, in a neat graphic
layout, each color photo with a name and the city
and state in which each victim had lived. These
were real people . . . people with lives and hopes
and dreams, dreams now never to be. I was standing
there in Walgreens completely shrouded in grief.
I had to collect myself.

No one knew who I was. No one cared. I was just a lady standing at the newspaper stand, sharing in America's collective grief. Others around the newsstand appeared somewhat emotional—but my tears were decidedly *different* and my grief was quite *personal*.

I ached inside. I prayed that God would be the comforter to me that I know Him to be. And I prayed for Todd's widow Lisa and their children—especially the baby who had not yet been welcomed into the world.

I drove home. That familiar feeling of numbness had returned in full force. All I could do was let the tears flow.

I've learned through this experience that tears aren't necessarily a bad thing. Tears keep us inextricably bound to our realities. They cleanse us, and allow us a channel whereby we can release our grief. Withholding tears can sometimes have a corrosive effect on our bodies and our spirits.

Through tears, we are able to "cast our cares" as God has asked us to do. I really didn't know that then, but I know now.

For the next few days, I could not function. It was as if my life as I'd known it was suspended in time. My husband Warren kept the house going. I tried to be the doting mother I'd always been to my children, but I found myself emotionally absent for a time. Absent—and frightened. I didn't want Warren to leave. If he was going to the store, I'd ask him, "When will you be back?"

I knew the Bible verse "They who sow in tears shall reap in joy and singing" (Psalm 126:5 AMP). But right then I could not imagine anything good coming from my suffering, or the sufferings of the family members of all those who perished aboard Flight 93. Certainly not joy or singing.

I could not imagine anything good coming from my suffering, or the sufferings of the family members of all those who perished aboard Flight 93.

I did not go to work for the next few days. I was bed-ridden, sleeping in my daughter's room so I could avoid the TV, which Warren was watching. I escaped my pain through sleep, and when I wasn't sleeping, I found myself unable to stop crying. I was inconsolable, afraid of the phone, afraid of the doorbell ringing, afraid of Warren leaving the house. My children said, "Mama, are you going to eat with us? Are you going to come and watch TV with us?"

And I felt violated. One Sunday we were getting ready for church and a TV news team was at the door. We wondered, *How could they just show up like this?*

One Sunday we were getting ready for church and a TV news team was at the door. We wondered, How could they just show up like this?

I went back to work, but nothing was normal. The media attention was constant. Federal authorities—an FBI agent, a United States attorney from Washington, and a representative from the New York Terrorist Task Force came to interview me in the police station in our town—and let me know that eventually I would be called on to testify in the Zacarias Moussaoui trial. Simply to talk to the authorities about such homeland-security issues was frightening and stressful.

Not only that, but *they* were concerned about *our* security in the fearful climate following 9/11. We—and our neighbors—noticed cars in our subdivision that didn't belong, but the FBI told us not to worry. They were taking care of us. We did, however, install an alarm system.

During October, when the anthrax scare was in the news, I received a letter from Europe. I wasn't sure what to do, so I gave it to the FBI. It turned out to be a letter from someone thanking me for my courage.

Through all this, our children, who were very young at the time, were responding pretty much like other young children after September 11th. At first they worried that the "bad people" were going to come and get them. My son in particular is very sensitive and inquisitive, and of course, people at school were talking about it. Warren and I were careful to sit down with them and explain, as much as we could, Mommy's role in what had happened. We wanted them to learn it from us—not the media.

WEEKS PASSED. I WAS BACK AT WORK, but life
was far from normal. My husband suggested I get
some help. So did my supervisors at Verizon, seeing
me in tears all the time. I knew it was time too.
I contacted Verizon's EAP (Employee Assistance
Program). They did all the paperwork and found
a professional fairly close to my home. I went into
therapy, not really knowing what to expect. I knew
I needed to talk to *someone*. I knew I was not able
to bear this burden alone.

Psychotherapy was not at all what I imagined.
I sat in a doctor's modestly furnished office, and I
was allowed—no, encouraged—to talk and talk.
This went on for about six months, twice a week in
one-hour sessions. I grieved Todd Beamer's loss as
if he were a family member. I shared my feelings
of stress over my work, the media attention, the
prospect of testifying at the Moussaoui trial, and my
sense that I had not asked for any of this.

I'm not sure what I was looking for, but the
sessions were different than I had expected. I wasn't
advised by my therapist in any way; nor was I
diagnosed with anything specific, such as the

condition commonly known as *post-traumatic stress syndrome*. She just listened.

In retrospect, I wondered whether the therapist was acting in my best interest. I mean, wasn't there something she could have told me to give me some guidance, coping mechanisms, or even just her professional opinion? Isn't that what therapists do?

In conjunction with my therapy sessions, I also received biblical counseling from my pastor, Ira J. Acree. He had been on vacation during 9/11 and, like so many travelers, became stranded; so we didn't talk right away, but in October I called him when the pressure and media attention did not go away. We prayed together, and our church on Chicago's West Side rallied around me. This was a tremendous help spiritually, as I slowly began to understand that God was using me in the midst of this tragedy.

BUT IT TOOK A LONG TIME.

As the months passed, I really thought the spotlight would fade, that the stress and activity would blow over. What happened was the opposite: When the nation marked the first anniversary of the national tragedy, Warren and I were in New York—

God, I was to learn, had more faith in me than I had in myself.

doing interviews. I began to receive various awards, which I appreciated; but they still reminded me of that terrible day when I was the last person to talk to a young husband and father who wondered "what do the hijackers want." My employer was pressuring me about what I was saying to the media *and* about handling my job—to the point where my husband and I had to engage an attorney. For a quiet, private person who has always shared her thoughts with close friends and family, the strain was intense.

Yet God, I was to learn, had more faith in me than I had in myself.

But I'm getting ahead of the story. . . .

called

CHAPTER EIGHT

FACE-TO-FACE

HOW DO THE MEDIA find you?

My home phone number, although unlisted, was passed from one media outlet to another. It was as though it had been posted somewhere in neon lights. My husband and I had to hire a liaison to help handle the barrage of inquiries—from local newspapers and radio stations, to international networks like the BBC. Prior to September 11th, my closest ties to the media were my big television in the family room, the radio in my car and at work, and the daily newspapers I read. That soon changed, dramatically.

My first television interview was with NBC *Dateline*'s Stone Phillips. After that came Court TV, *Larry King Live,* CNN, CBS, ABC, A&E, and a host of others. They all wanted me to recount my conversation with Todd Beamer.

I was not media-savvy. I was nervous at first, but I spoke with a quiet confidence that God was using me. With each subsequent interview I became bolder, telling each interviewer about my faith in God, and how I believe He scheduled my "appointment" with Todd Beamer.

With each subsequent interview I became bolder, telling each interviewer about my faith in God.

When I think of how that Verizon operator turned that call over to me . . . when I think of how my husband was there, ready to support me when I got off the phone . . . even, as strange as it may seem, when I think of my having the same name as Todd's wife . . . I know in my heart that this was all orchestrated by God. God is a God of order. He is meticulous in planning and detail, and He's much too big and purposeful for coincidence. I believe He knew I'd need support. I believe He gave me a compelling message for anyone seeking to know God's purpose for them.

And God knew Lisa Beamer would need to be surrounded by the love of family and that she needed to be lifted up through the prayers of the faithful. She and I spoke a number of times, and we wanted to meet. Neither of us had any idea how soon that would come about.

I RECEIVED A CALL FROM the *Oprah Winfrey Show*. Lisa Beamer also got a call. A producer asked if we'd both consent to a live television interview. Sounds simple enough, right? But there was one caveat: Lisa Beamer and I had never met in person, and neither of us was willing to fly . . . given the September 11th tragedy.

Lisa and I had our misgivings. We wanted to meet on our own. She, understandably, was terribly afraid to fly, but fortunately for me, I learned the show would air in Chicago. I live in a suburb just south of Chicago.

Ms. Winfrey, understanding Lisa Beamer's fears, personally made travel arrangements for her. She assured Lisa the journey would be safe.

And so that October, the two Lisas finally met face-to-face. Lisa Beamer had not yet had her baby—she was due in January. We met in one of the Harpo Studio "green rooms," where guests wait before going on the air, and there she was, this blonde petite woman with an angelic face. We embraced and we cried. Neither of us could speak, we were so overcome with emotion.

The studio audience only got a snapshot of our collective testimony. Somewhere between time constraints and commercials, we managed to tell our story, and the audience responded. There were nodding heads, and tearstained cheeks, and a wonderful outpouring of empathy for Lisa Beamer. After the show I met Todd's older sister, Melissa.

It is clear to me now that God had ordered both Lisa's and my footsteps. People the world over need to hear this incredible story of faith . . . and they need to hear it now!

Lisa and I try to keep in touch. She is seeking

to live a low-profile existence, out of the media glare, and I respect and understand that. She's busy raising her three babies, and I'm busy with my family, my ministry, helping as I can toward raising funds for a permanent memorial to the heroes of Flight 93 (see page 147), and thinking about what might be next—perhaps work in the medical field.

Yet as we look back on the searing events of September 11th, I realize that *many* of us touched by that day can't go back to the way it was "before." I also keep in touch with some of the families who lost loved ones in Flight 93; they too have been forever changed. (Some of their stories can be found in the back of this book.) In the news, debates go on and on about keeping our airports and seaports safe, about how to deal with Islamic extremism, about our Mideast policy. The Moussaoui trial brought back the horror of that day. Even as we observe the five-year mark, September 11, 2001, is still very much with us. It will *always* be with me.

As I've said, there is much good that can come out of our collective sorrow. I've learned a lot from my experiences—and I'd like to share some of that with you, in the hope that you might be inspired to take on your own "assignment."

called

CHAPTER NINE

ARE YOU READY?

WHEN I WAS GOING THROUGH COUNSELING with my pastor, one of the things he said to me that really left an impression is that God is more concerned about our *availability* than He is our *ability*. He grants us skills and talents, to be sure. But what God wants most of all—what He wanted from Jacob, from Joseph, from Moses, from Samuel, from David, from Esther; what He wanted from Mary the mother of Jesus, and Martha and Paul and Peter and so many more—what He wants is for us to say, "Lord, here I am—I'm ready!"

In churches all over the world, songs are sung by believers proclaiming a steadfast faith in God, and a willingness to serve Him no matter what! Those are powerful words and powerful promises we make, but are we really willing to be called?

Are we *available* to be called, or are we so wrapped up in our own earthly desires, goals, and accomplishments that we have little time to pay more than lip service to our desire to live with purpose, passion, and commitment?

After a few therapy sessions and much prayer and fasting, I found myself not only able to cope with my new pressures, but I believe I was imbued with a new insight that would enable me to speak boldly for my Lord, and bear witness of His mercy and grace in the coming weeks and months. However, I must admit: I don't think my life will ever be the same. I see everything in a different light now. Some things remain routine for me, but I carry them out with a greater fervency and with more deliberation. Every morning when I wake up, I still start my day with prayer and meditation. I thank God for the dawning of a new day, and I thank Him that His mercies are new every morning.

Before I leave home I make sure I kiss everyone good-bye, one at a time. One can never know if it will be the last time you see your family. September 11th made me keenly aware of that.

My husband Warren and I pray together, and we pray *with* our children. We want to be careful to teach them to acknowledge God in their lives—and to impart to them a spirit of gratitude.

I am no longer in professional therapy, but the door remains open for additional sessions, should that become necessary. God has transformed me from a wife and working mother to an ambassador for Christ. I am a witness that *God will equip you with whatever skills you need to carry out His work.* Todd Beamer needed the reassurance of a fellow follower of Christ. God promises us that if we believe . . . He'll be with us to the very end. Even in death. I believe God kept His promise to Todd. God used me to speak peace and comfort to Todd, even as he was approaching the sunset of his young life.

I am a witness that God will equip you with whatever skills you need to carry out His work.

In November of 2003, I met Todd Beamer's parents, David and Peggy Beamer, and his sister Michele for the first time. We agreed to gather at a popular banquet hall in Glen Ellyn, Illinois. It was a cold, crisp evening. Warren accompanied me to a dinner the Beamers invited us to attend, sponsored by the school Todd attended as a child.

I remember being a bit nervous as I got dressed in a brown pantsuit. Warren and I had arrived at the banquet hall about fifteen minutes before Todd's parents walked in. Once they arrived, we were all escorted to a private room. We were able to converse freely and without interruption for about a half hour. Todd's parents were very warm, and had a few questions for me. We went over the conversation I had with Todd during his last moments aboard Flight 93. They also reminisced, sharing fond memories of the days when they lived in Illinois. Mr. Beamer and Michele were the keynote speakers that evening. After dinner we took pictures, talked a little more, and hugged. And we've kept in touch.

I was reminded again several months later of my September 11th experience when in May of 2004 I received a phone call from the National

Commission on Terrorist Attacks. Officials with this agency wanted to confirm information they'd gathered from previous interviews. I fully cooperated, as I'd done before—aware that my life had undergone a great change.

I never pictured myself as a public speaker, but through the grace of God, I've become one, and I now travel around the country to community groups and civic organizations—talking to people about serving God, about helping their fellow human beings, about their *significance*—even as "ordinary women and men." In 2003 I received the "Person of the Year" award from the American Red Cross and spoke about—and to—"ordinary heroes."

But really, no one is ordinary! If you've ever wondered what God's purpose is for your life, just ask Him. The Bible tells us, *"There is nothing covered that will not be revealed"* (Matthew 10:26 NKJV).

I believe we each are here to bring God glory, and I believe that God uses situations and circumstances to mold us and to conform us into His image . . . like a potter shapes and molds clay. Being on the spinning wheel can sometimes be dizzying. Sometimes bits of clay fall off the wheel to the floor in moist clumps of nothingness, and sometimes the pressure of becoming pliable in the Potter's hands is painful—but the end result is a beautiful vessel that can be used mightily by God, to strengthen, to edify, to encourage, to instill hope and trust . . . and to ultimately bear witness of God's awesome power and wonder.

Surrendering all takes time. But surrender your will to His. Give Him all your doubts and fears. Don't worry about your inadequacies, because as I've learned, you really can do *all things through God.*

And God has an assignment for you that only *you* can fulfill. When we begin to turn off our DVDs and CDs, radios, televisions, and other distractions, and dedicate some quality time to spend that time alone with God, we will be better able to understand His character . . . and He will reveal His will to us.

Think about it. To whom do you tell your secrets? I'll bet your answer would be: only to your closest friends and confidantes . . . people you enjoy spending time with, right? And so it is with our Father God. We can't know His heart and His plan for us if we don't spend time seeking Him, away from the noise, away from the distractions we all have. The Bible tells us, if we draw near to Him, He'll draw near to us.

You might be wondering, *How can I be prepared to be used by God?* I can't answer that question. I don't think anyone can. But I believe each day we live our eulogies. Each life experience, bitter or sweet, is part of our training and preparation for the future. God may need you to intervene in a situation that will require your specific skill set. Perhaps you're an expert in your field, a health-care professional, an engineer, a swimming instructor, a person skilled in politics and diplomacy, an attorney who specializes in a rare area of practice, an athlete whose strong muscles are needed to lift an object to free someone . . . or perhaps you have already lived through a horrific experience and can help get someone else through their suffering.

Each life experience, bitter or sweet, is part of our training and preparation for the future.

All the innocents aboard Flight 93 met their end, fighting. Although we can't know exactly what happened in those final moments over southwestern Pennsylvania, I do believe Todd and some of his fellow passengers broke into that cockpit. And their refusal to remain frozen in fear and simply resigned to their violent fate more than likely prevented an even greater catastrophe that certainly could have claimed even more lives—and destroyed some priceless symbols of our great country. Flight 93, from everything I've studied, was headed for Washington—possibly even the White House or the Capitol Building! They fought back, sacrificing their own lives and saving scores of others. Even in tragedy, they all had *purpose.*

There are a myriad of ways in which we can all be used by the hand of God. I believe, in fact, we *are* His hands, His eyes, His heart. And we see that in action when we act as servants to each other. When we lend to those who need to borrow. When we lift someone who is at her wit's end. When we feed those who are hungry. When we offer our friendship in the midst of someone's intense loneliness. When we are able to empathize with someone who has lost his job. When we can help that person find work. We can provide comfort to the lost and hurting only if we're willing and available.

I don't know what your special "assignment" might be—or when you might be called upon in the midst of your everyday life to be a hero. I don't know how you will prepare for that challenge. I do think that God uses us as we are, with our unique gifts, abilities, experiences. For example, I guess I've always been a good listener, and I've been told I have good judgment and can take charge when necessary. Warren has said that when he first met me, he was struck by the way family and friends were always calling asking for my advice.

But even with that, I wasn't prepared on September 11th. Like Todd Beamer, I simply went on in faith. I didn't have time to be scared. I was just thinking about Todd.

I would also say this. When you find yourself confronted by a crisis, a loss, some difficult emotional problem: *Don't panic!* It's easy to fall apart in a crisis.

After September 11th there was a new sense of national resolve and purpose, a new feeling that life has value.

This sounds obvious . . . and hard to do. But think about it. Think about situations you've had when you've fallen apart. Did it help? Probably not. But when crises come, if we remain calm *and* trust God, we will be a lot more able to meet those challenges.

We've talked some about lessons from September 11. It is easy to forget how *unified* we were following those tragic events. How in the days after flags popped up on front porches and automobile antennae, there was a new sense of national resolve and purpose, a new feeling that life has value.

Maybe we need to get back to that.

The next time you think *your* life has no meaning or purpose, think again. God shows no partiality (Acts 10:34 NKJV). He loves all of us the same—and yet He loves each of us uniquely, just as He made each of us uniquely! But no matter what your age, your race, your cultural or economic walk of life, your life has meaning and significance, far beyond anything you can imagine. God is just waiting for you to respond.

Will you?

EPILOGUE

THE SUNDAY AFTER THE TOWERS FELL
and the planes crashed, churches across
America were packed. Many people
experienced a crisis of faith following
the tragedy. The lingering question that
robbed many people of sleep: *Where was
God?* Shortly after September 11th, I
received a poignant piece from a friend.
You may have even seen it yourself. It
addresses that very question. I now share
it with you in the hope that it will give
you strength, open the eyes of your
understanding, and give you peace.

WHERE WAS I?

You say where was I?

I was on the 110th floor in a smoke-filled room with a man who called his wife to say good-bye.

I held his fingers steady as he dialed.

I gave him the peace to say, "Honey, I am not going to make it, but it's okay . . . I'm ready to go."

I was with his wife when he called as she fed breakfast to their children. I held her up as she tried to understand his words and as she realized he really wasn't coming home that night.

I was in the stairwell of the 23rd floor when a woman cried out to Me for help, for the very first time in her life. "I have been knocking on the door of your heart for fifty years!" I said. "Of course I will show you the way home— only believe in Me now."

I was at the base of the building with the chaplain ministering to the injured and devastated souls. I took him home to tend to his flock in heaven. He heard My voice and answered.

I was on all four of those planes, in every seat, with every prayer. I was with the crew as they were overtaken. I was in the very hearts of the believers there, comforting and assuring them that their faith had saved them.

I was in Texas, Kansas, London . . . I was everywhere. I was standing next to you when you heard the terrible news. Did you sense Me?

I want you to know that I saw every face. I knew every name—though not all knew Me. Some met Me for the first time on the 86th floor. Some sought Me with their very last breath. Some couldn't hear Me calling to them through the smoke and flames, "Come to Me, this way . . . take my hand." Some had never heard My voice before. And a few chose, for the final time, to ignore Me.

But I was there.

I did not place you in the Tower that day. You may not know why, but I do. However, if you were there in that explosive moment in time, would you have reached for Me?

September 11th, 2001, was not the end of the journey for you. But someday your journey will end. And I will be there for you as well. Seek Me now while I may be found. Then, at any moment, you'll know you are ready to go.

I will be in the stairwell of your final moments.

Love, God

Author Unknown

LETTERS TO LISA

"I Wonder If God
Called Upon Me
to Do His Work,
Would I Be Willing?"

*Lisa Jefferson has received letters and
e-mails from around the world. Here's
a sampling from those whose lives were
touched by her story and message.*

I OFTEN WONDER IF GOD called upon me to do His work, would I be willing? Would I come through? . . . Thank you for being where you needed to be that day. God works in many ways, and He chose you!

I GAVE YOU A TOUR OF THE U.S. CAPITOL. As someone who was saved [from the possible destruction of the Capitol], it was truly an honor to meet you and a privilege to show you the building that you were a part of saving.

Since we met, I switched jobs and moved back home to Illinois. I realized that I had been given an incredible second chance to live my life in the way it should be lived.

YOU ARE A SHINING EXAMPLE of all that is good and decent about America.

YOU HAVE PERFORMED A TRUE PUBLIC SERVICE—not just to the unfortunate caller and his family, but to the entire country. We so badly need the reassurance that there are yet caring people like yourself who will go the extra step to render aid and comfort in these difficult times.

I AM SURE THAT YOU PROVIDED COMFORT to Mr. Beamer in his final minutes of life and that he knew that his love and final thoughts would be communicated to his family through you.

EVERY TIME I FLY, I imagine that conversation, and it helps me get through each flight. I will never forget your calming spirit.

MONTHS AFTER THE DAY, we continue to be touched by your kind and caring demeanor. I consider myself to be particularly blessed. As one of your former English teachers at Fenger High School, I am especially elated, knowing that you matured into a beautiful and inspirational soul. I am proud of you.

Janell A. Taylor

'ALWAYS REMEMBER':
STORIES FROM FLIGHT 93 FAMILIES

I invited families of Flight 93 heroes to share some of their lives and thoughts now. Some of the responses follow.

FROM PEGGY BEAMER, MOTHER OF TODD:

"Always Remember, and Always Say a Prayer"

IT'S BEEN NEARLY FIVE YEARS SINCE 9/11, nearly 1,800 days since we lost our loved ones on Flight 93— those who banded together to launch our first counterattack (a successful one) on the first day of battle in this new world war. We cherish their memory, and while many forget what happened or pretend the difficult days will just go away, we recall the events, the images, and the actions of that day every day. We know that the brave actions of the passengers and crew of Flight 93 serve as an American example of the kind of courage and sacrifice required to protect our freedoms.

What a special blessing "The Call" has been to the Beamer family and our fellow Americans. "Let's roll!" was a call to action and a signal to the Flight 93 team to launch the counterattack. Just seeing those words on the wall at Walter Reed Army Hospital to encourage some of our wounded soldiers is also a blessing. We are thankful that Lisa Jefferson was there on the phone for Todd and to add details about what the passengers and crew of Flight 93 planned to do— and did do. It helps to know.

Todd and Lisa's children, David, Drew, and Morgan, are all doing well. The boys are active little guys, involved in sports and church activities. Morgan is in preschool and is an outgoing, gregarious little girl. Todd is missed—remembered every day—and we continue to talk to his children about him, his character, what he did when he was their age.

We carry on and we miss Todd beyond what words can say. Always remember and always say a prayer for those leading, serving, protecting, and sacrificing.

FROM DEBORAH BORZA, MOTHER OF DEORA BODLEY:

"From This Moment On, I Will Be Loving"

WHILE WAITING FOR A CALL FROM UNITED,
waiting to find out if my daughter was on Flight 93,
I went across the street from work to wait in a church.
I went inside, placed my cell phone on the pew, and
asked God, "You are the only One who knows where
Deora is. Where is she?" And I heard a voice say,
"She's with Me." And just after hearing that, my
phone rang. "Hello, Ms. Borza?" "Yes." "This is
Sharon Dewitt from United. I'm sorry to inform you
that your daughter, Deora Bodley, was a passenger on
board United Flight 93, which crashed outside—"

I burst out screaming, "My baby, my baby!"
And those people who were in the church came
running over to me, bringing me water, trying to help.
I tried to brush them away; I remember thinking,
What good is all this? Then I heard a voice saying,
"Look around you." I looked around and saw all these
people, just wanting to make some kind of difference
for me in my time of sadness. And I said to them,
"I am so sorry. In trying to be tough, refusing your

kindness, I didn't really see what you were wanting to do for me. Please forgive me and know from this moment on I will be courageous and loving for the rest of my life."

I've learned of so many people who were inspired by Deora. An eleven-year-old boy started a book-donation project in honor of Deora, called Read All Over. A college student created a program called Project Team, where volunteers give their time to middle-school students, teaching them team-building skills. He had read about Deora and was moved to do something in her memory. A young pregnant woman called to ask if she had a girl, could she name her Deora. She had read about Deora and fallen in love with her, and she wanted her baby to have Deora's name. (She did have a girl—and the child was born on Deora's birthday, April 8.)

There are more stories like these. I'm glad I listened—and accepted the task I was given, to encourage people to *make a difference.*

"To Make Something Special Come from Her Loss"

WHEN WE BECAME A BLENDED FAMILY of four children, we went down on our knees in prayer and felt that God was calling us to our "mission field"—our four children entering their teenage years. Well, it was not only a huge job but a very challenging and rewarding one! One thing that we felt was so important was to let every individual child know how much we loved them and how proud we were of them.

The importance of our "calling" became apparent on September 11, 2001, when our beloved 21-year-old daughter, Nicole Carol Miller, was murdered on Flight 93 with thirty-nine other lost loved ones. We both had peace that Nicole not only knew what to do in her time of danger but that she knew in her heart that we loved her so much and were so very proud of her. During our time of overwhelming grief and pain, we had the peace that because we did what God had called us to do, we had no regrets over our life with Nicole. She knew we loved her, and we knew how much she loved us.

Since that fateful day we lost our lovely daughter, we have felt that God has called us once again. This time our calling is to do "good" in Nicole's memory; to make something wonderfully special come from her loss and the loss of the other thirty-nine loved ones aboard Flight 93.

We have both worked on the Flight 93 National Memorial (see page 147) since the beginning of the process and are still involved in it.

We championed a scholarship in Nicole's honor at her school, West Valley College in Saratoga, California, started by her fellow students. Our efforts brought in donations from friends, family, and companies that made the scholarship into an annual endowment. There have been two deserving recipients since its inception.

In our town of Chico, California, we were involved in efforts to plant a "September 11th Memorial Grove" in our local park. In 2003 a rose was named after Nicole. In April 2006 the "Remember Me" rose program dedicated the official Flight 93 rose "Forty Heroes" in a ceremony in New York City.

We will never forget our "little love bug" and the impact she had on our lives. The lessons we have learned throughout our struggle through her loss will be carried on throughout our lives, and we will continue to do "good" in Nicole's memory.

"The World Needs to Know"

A PIECE OF MY HEART will be broken forever. Although the pain is still well alive, I'm now finding reason to smile and laugh again. When I think of her love and sweet memories I can smile, for I was blessed to have the pleasure of being her mother for her brief existence on this earth.

Nicole touched many lives and still continues to touch lives through her memorial Web site. I have met many wonderful people from around the world through her Web site. What has helped me get through this tragedy the most is being able to talk about Nicole. I always ask, "What would she want?" I can feel a mother's pain of losing a child and can help those who have had to experience similar tragedies. I have met many grieving mothers since September 11th and believe that now I can help those who are hurting get through their pain—if only to be there and listen.

We will overcome that September day by doing something positive for our loved ones. Honoring them with the Flight 93 Memorial will show their incredible act of courage and sacrifice. The passengers and crew all had an important choice to make. They could have sat there and done as the terrorists told them, in hopes they would have lived—or they could have chosen to sacrifice themselves, fighting for the safety of their fellow Americans and giving themselves for the greater cause. Because of their act of courage, the terrorists did not complete their mission. The world needs to know who each and every one of the brave souls of Flight 93 are and of their heroic acts that saved the lives of many.

"Last Hope"

On that tragic day of nine-eleven,
Three thousand lives lost on earth,
gained in heaven

Many of us were going on with our days,
Living our lives our own selfish ways

The terrorists had a plan,
To kill as many Americans as they can

With Flight 11, 175, and 77,
They struck the World Trade Center
and the Pentagon, shaking the heavens

There was terror in the streets and in our homes,
Buildings falling, blood, remains, and broken bones

Just as we thought the terrorists
had successfully completed their plans,
There was one *last hope,* one final stand

Flight 93 was on its course,
When the terrorists tried to take over
with barbaric force,

Forty passengers and crew on that flight,
The strangers bonded together and decided to fight

Knowing that death would be their final fate,
They gathered, they fought for the
Freedom of the United States

Stopping the terrorists from reaching their
intended destination,
They won the first fight,
it didn't break the heart of our nation

The battle ended in the fields of
Shanksville, Pennsylvania,
Not the word Allah, nor fear of death could tame them

True heroes are the passengers and crew of Flight 93,
A symbol of America, *The Land of the Free!*

Written in loving memory of my sister,
and true hero of Flight 93,
Nicole Carol Miller

Forever your sister, Tiffney Miller

"I Just Want to Tell You I Love You"

MARK BINGHAM DIED WITH TODD BEAMER and a group of brave passengers fighting terrorists aboard Flight 93. As United Airlines flight attendants, my sister, Candyce Hoglan, and I have become advocates for improved aviation security, petitioning the federal government and the airlines to commit to higher standards of security for the flying public. I also write and speak on issues of terrorism and Muslim/Western relations.

Mark and Todd Beamer were schoolmates and athletes at Los Gatos High School in the San Francisco Bay area, graduating one year apart. Mark was a rugby player, and I now host the biennial Bingham Cup of rugby. Deena Burnett, widow of Tom Burnett, another Flight 93 hero, and I cosponsored the inaugural "Run to Remember" in San Francisco on September 11, 2005.

I am grateful to have received a telephone call from Mark aboard Flight 93 minutes before he, Todd, and others charged down that narrow 757 aisle. Mark told his family: "I just want to tell you I love you."

FROM MARY LOUISE WHITE,
MOTHER OF HONOR ELIZABETH WAINIO:

"She Brought Me out of the Fog"

ON SEPTEMBER 11, 2001, I wanted to die. On October 9, 2001, I was introduced to three people who would help me live.

Standing in the first makeshift memorial just outside the crash site, I met two women and a nine-year-old. We spoke for approximately fifteen minutes, and then they invited my husband and me to Shanksville to see the memorial they placed there. They asked about communicating with me; one had pictures she wanted to share, and I gratefully obliged with my home address.

After returning to Florida, my pain only worsened. Remembering the beauty through the horror, I wrote a letter to the editor to try to thank everyone for all they tried to do and were doing. Then I retreated from life. My poor husband. We were married only five years and he didn't know what to do. The doctors prescribed different medications and I existed, not lived.

Late October 2001, I received a large envelope from one of the women I had met that October day. As I opened it, I cried, laughed, and smiled. Her nine-year-old niece had gone back to her school and said she met me and heard how my daughter was my little "Woodstock," like the bird in *Peanuts*. She asked her fourth-grade classmates to "help make Mrs. White not so sad." Here were twenty cards, handmade and decorated with drawings of Woodstock, and a lovely note from their teacher. I wrote her immediately to thank her, but soon I went back into my shell.

The letters and pictures kept coming. My first return to Shanksville was in April for Arbor Day to plant a tree in her yard with the help of the Shanksville VFD. We also planted a tree at her niece's school and gave her class a pizza party to thank them for being so kind. The children encircled the tree and we held hands. Then we went inside for pizza and they sang "Beacons of Hope" to me and presented me with yellow roses, my daughter's favorite (which they had no way of knowing). Pictures, letters, and notes continued. I went in September for the first anniversary and then in October for my daughter's birthday, and my new friend was always available. She was my Velcro friend, sticking to me ever so lightly, just enough so I knew she was there.

We exchanged visits, and each trip we got closer. Each trip there was easier. I actually smiled at some point. We talked often, e-mailed even more often, and then the news came: kidney cancer, spread to the lungs.

I soon stopped feeling sorry for myself. Here was a young woman who had given me her friendship and her compassion, and now she had this horrible diagnosis. It seemed like our friendship had lasted decades, not months. She and I thought the same; we liked the same things. She could *not* be dying. I had lost my only daughter—I couldn't lose my new friend.

As she fought hard to live, we grew even closer and continued to exchange visits. I called her every day. She died in July 2005, not quite four years after we first met. She brought me out of the fog and back into the light. I am still grieving and trying to find my way. Strange how tragedy can bring people who might otherwise not meet to a place where they can call each other "friend."

FROM BARBARA AND LARRY CATUZZI,
PARENTS OF LAUREN GRANDCOLAS:

"You Can Do It"

AFTER SEPTEMBER 11, 2001, our family established a foundation called The Lauren Catuzzi Grandcolas Foundation. We have been very excited to be able to honor Lauren in this positive manner, and we think that she would have loved what we have accomplished so far. Our mission is to provide health, education, and welfare to women and children.

Lauren was writing a book for women encouraging them to expand their horizons and learn new things for a richer life, with children, husbands, family, and friends.

Lauren's sisters, Vaughn Lohec and Dara Near, with the incredible help and guidance of our publisher, Chronicle Books, finished her book, which is called *You Can Do It*.

It has been very well received and proceeds will go to the foundation.

In addition, the foundation has funded two neonatal units at hospitals in Houston and in Marin County, California, and has also provided assistance to a hospital in North Carolina. The balance of foundation activities has involved the awarding of scholarships to young women around the country who are about to enter their first year of college.

The family and board of the foundation feel that taking a positive approach regarding this tragedy would be exactly what Lauren would expect of us. She set the bar for us in many aspects of living and achieving, and it was our strongest desire to follow her spirit and zest for life.

FROM CAROLE O'HARE, DAUGHTER OF HILDA MARCIN:

"By Helping Others, I Can Find Peace"

AFTER MY MOTHER WAS tragically murdered on United Airlines Flight 93, September 11, 2001, I felt that my life, too, had ended. There are no words that come to mind that describe the pain, anger, sadness, frustration, and gut-wrenching feelings that a person experiences during such a traumatic event.

My dear mother, Hilda Marcin, was a lady who loved life, even though she, too, suffered a number of tragedies during her lifetime. She lost three brothers due to childhood illnesses; she immigrated to the United States when she was eight years old not speaking a word of English, having to stay back in school three times until she mastered the language well enough to move forward. Never did she falter—never did she fail. Hilda always rose up like the stars above; always shining brightly no matter how the clouds formed or how stormy they became. She was my lifelong inspiration and friend.

Because Hilda was moving to California from New Jersey on September 11, 2001, she and I had planned many exciting things to do together like volunteering, gardening, and traveling. I can still to this day feel the softness of her fingertips as we would recite the Lord's Prayer, knowing that this tiny, gentle lady with a heart of gold had a fiery spirit and strong will that led her through some turbulent times. Yet that softness of her fingertips yielded the sense that through it all, she never hardened, never was bitter, always remained even-tempered and loving to those around her.

After the first anniversary of 9/11, I took it upon myself to start writing a newsletter for the families—every month, without fail. I needed to do something connected to the tragedy, yet I was not sure where to begin. I found that writing about my experience helped me feel better, writing about my mother even more so, and connecting to the other family members gave me a sense of belonging and hope because at that point, my healing and my strength emanated from them; we shared a common tragedy and we shared the great desire to heal. A bonding between us has taken place, as they share with me their stories of inspiration and hope, and how they have turned a terrible tragedy into doing good things for others.

Nearly five years later, I am still the conduit to the families, and I still get my strength from them; their beautiful notes to me, their thank-you messages, and their stories of how they are healing and moving on with their lives, even though it is so difficult at times. The newsletter also provides them with avenues where they can find support groups, books on grief, financial assistance, Web sites, and any information that can help them in their own lives. My hope is that by helping others, I can find peace in my own life, and look ahead to better things for the future. So far, it is working.

I have always had a strong faith in God, always believed that we all have a purpose that is predestined for us, challenges to face, and tasks to accomplish. Keeping my "new family" connected and together has been my task and my challenge. Even five years later, there are days when I wonder how long I can keep doing this. Then I suddenly wake up and realize, "Wow, if my mom and the other passengers and crew members could face what they faced for a very long forty minutes of their lives, then I certainly can do this very safe, comfortable task on behalf of all of them." It's the least I can do.

As Eleanor Roosevelt once said, "You gain strength, courage, and confidence by every experience in which you really stop to look fear in the face. You are able to say to yourself, 'I have lived through this horror. I can take the next thing that comes along.' You must do the thing you think you cannot do."

'A FIELD OF HONOR':
THE FLIGHT 93 NATIONAL MEMORIAL

On September 24, 2002, Congress passed the Flight 93 National Memorial Act. The Act created a new national park unit to "commemorate the passengers and crew of Flight 93 who, on September 11, 2001, courageously gave their lives, thereby thwarting a planned attack on our Nation's Capital." The memorial will be developed near Shanksville, Pennsylvania, where Flight 93 crashed on September 11, 2001.

When completed, Flight 93 National Memorial will encompass 2,200 acres. The memorial design was selected by a group comprising family members, community representatives, and design professionals. The memorial's mission statement declares, "A Common Field One Day, a Field of Honor Forever. May all who visit this place remember the collective acts of courage and sacrifice of the passengers and crew, revere this hallowed ground as the final resting place of those heroes, and reflect on the power of individuals who choose to make a difference."

For more information or to donate to the memorial, visit www.flight93memorialproject.org.

A SPECIAL THANKS

Sherrill Chidiac
Born January 23, 1942
Passed Away April 10, 2005

For Sherrill, who never stopped believing this book would be published. Her faith in the impact of my story fueled this project in ways that are almost inexplicable. Even in death, her spirit of hope, her kindness, and her concern for the human condition lives on. Thank you, Sherrill, for adding great value to the process of writing this book. We believe you're pleased with the outcome.

Lisa and Felicia

ABOUT THE AUTHORS

LISA D. JEFFERSON is an inspirational speaker, wife, and mother of two. She lives in the Chicago area with her husband, Warren, son, Warren II, and daughter, Lonye'. She has received numerous awards, including "Person of the Year" from the American Red Cross. Currently she is involved in fund-raising efforts for the Flight 93 National Memorial Project. *Called* is her first book.

FELICIA MIDDLEBROOKS is one of the top media personalities in Chicago. She is co-anchor for the award-winning morning-drive program on CBS Radio/WBBM Newsradio 780 and has been honored by scores of organizations, receiving the coveted Edward R. Murrow Award for Excellence in News. She is also a filmmaker—her documentary, *Somebody's Child: The Redemption of Rwanda,* took top honors at a New York film festival in 2005.